HAFIZ ORACLE

Divine Guidance for a Blissful Life

RASSOULI

HAFIZ ORACLE
Divine Guidance for a Blissful Life

Copyright © 2025 Rassouli

All rights reserved. Other than for personal use, no part of these cards or this book may be reproduced in any way, in whole or part, without the written consent of the copyright holder or publisher. This publication is intended for spiritual and emotional guidance only. The content is not intended to replace medical assistance or treatment. The views and opinions expressed by the author, both within and outside of this publication, do not necessarily reflect the views of the publisher.

Published by Blue Angel Publishing®
10 Trafford Court, Wheelers Hill,
Victoria, Australia 3150
E-mail: info@blueangelonline.com
Website: www.blueangelonline.com

Edited by Cherise Asmah and Jules Sutherland

Blue Angel is a registered trademark of Blue Angel Gallery Pty Ltd.

ISBN: 978-1-922574-27-5

Printed on sustainably sourced paper,
with soy-based ink.

CONTENTS

HAFIZ: A GUIDE TO BEAUTY AND FREEDOM	7
THE MYSTERY OF HAFIZ	17
An Oracle for Humankind	23
The Tongue of the Hidden	25
Using These Cards	28
CARD MESSAGES	31
Song of Abundance	32
Song of Assurance	34
Song of Attraction	36
Song of Awakening	38
Song of Beauty	40
Song of Celebration	42
Song of Challenge	44
Song of Change	46
Song of Communion	48
Song of Courage	50
Song of Creation	52
Song of Desire	54
Song of Determination	56
Song of Dreams	58
Song of Faith	60
Song of Flow	62
Song of Forgiveness	64

Song of Freedom	**66**
Song of Friendship	**68**
Song of Gratitude	**70**
Song of Guidance	**72**
Song of Happiness	**74**
Song of Harmony	**76**
Song of Honesty	**78**
Song of Hope	**80**
Song of Humility	**82**
Song of Intimacy	**84**
Song of Joy	**86**
Song of Leisure	**88**
Song of Life	**90**
Song of Longing	**92**
Song of Love	**94**
Song of Nature	**96**
Song of Optimism	**98**
Song of Perseverance	**100**
Song of Play	**102**
Song of Power	**104**
Song of Presence	**106**
Song of Rebirth	**108**
Song of Relief	**110**
Song of Silence	**112**
Song of Success	**114**
Song of Surrender	**116**
Song of Uniqueness	**118**
ABOUT THE AUTHOR & ARTIST	**120**

HAFIZ: A GUIDE TO BEAUTY AND FREEDOM

Come and dwell with Hafiz
in a new advent, a new beginning,
to make room in your heart
for the arrival of a love far beyond
your hopes and dreams.
Light the candles with the flame of hope.
Light them with the burning
of the longing within your heart.
Hafiz, the Oracle of love,
waits for the opening of your heart
to come rushing in like a river
to fill you with the divine wine,
and to touch you with
the light of love.

HAFIZ has been the most influential guide in my life. He has spiritually held my hand, and has guided my journey along the path of freedom through a rose garden.

My spiritual connection with Hafiz started early in life when I first heard Sufis singing and dancing to his mystical songs. The verses were musical, rhythmic, and melodic. They were about love, beauty, and joy. With the help of my Sufi uncle, I memorized many of his songs and enjoyed singing the verses as my nursery rhymes. I began feeling Hafiz through my emotions rather than my intellect. His songs were not like lessons in school. They were playful and were filled with wonderful humor. Singing his songs from an early age was a total experience of bliss for me.

I learned from Hafiz to become a painter of beauty. I was led by the poetry of Hafiz to live freely with joy to find who I am, to listen to my heart, to laugh, to create, and to experience my life as my art. I am happier today than I have ever been in my life, and the wonder of this gift flows from Hafiz — and from the guidance embedded in who he is. This allows me to be free. He is a wonderful companion and spiritual friend. I could talk about my mystical experiences with Hafiz, but that would be for another time and place. My book, *Rumi Revealed*, describes some of the influences that Rumi—who lived a century before Hafiz—had on him.

Throughout my life, I have shared Hafiz with my friends, fans, and students. The images in my paintings are mostly influenced by the way Hafiz refers to the beings in his songs. They are untouchable in the physical realm because they are spiritual in nature. They are goddesses and angels who appear only in the imagination. I have learned from Hafiz to inspire others to experience the light of their own beings and to find their own uniqueness. I have learned from Hafiz to create artworks and writings as a fusion of life with art and the heart, thus, I called this process Fusionart.

As a dedicated follower of Hafiz, I have spent over 25 years—off and on—pursuing a continuing and committed effort to translate his mystical songs from Persian to English. It was truly a challenge. The book was published by Blue Angel Publishing under the title *Hafiz: Wisdom of Madness* in 2019, and it won the gold COVR award as the best poetry book in 2022. The popularity of Hafiz during the past two decades in the Western world has inspired me to translate some of the key empowering spiritual impressions of Hafiz for English-speaking readers in more detail. This idea led me to create the present deck of Hafiz oracle cards. It is my dream to inspire those who are interested to know his beautiful soul and awaken to what a wonderful guide and friend he can be if we open our hearts to him.

The songs of Hafiz reflected in these cards are gateways to the depth of his poetry. Each one of these songs has been taken from the poems found in the accompanying book, *Hafiz: Wisdom of Madness*. All the images and the interpretations have evolved through the heart as I have immersed myself in each verse of Hafiz as the Oracle. This set is a contribution toward building a connection that brings a glimpse of the deeper peace and joy that is possible. You receive it when you open the portal to your heart and develop the longing to express your own inner dreams. The kingdom is within you; I'm hoping that you will awaken to this truth.

Allow Hafiz to exalt you to a level of feeling that will enable you to express the uniqueness of who you are. Let his wisdom and empowering presence as an Oracle wash over you like the soft, gentle rain of caressing love and kindness. Take his songs inside as your guide to discover what it means to be fully human. Behold when the light of a pure love comes into your world — everything will change.

As you go through these cards, Hafiz will help to illuminate your true self. Put your logical mind aside and allow this divine Oracle to open and permeate your heart, and he will show the joy of existence as you live in the sanctuary of your own light and being.

My hope is that you might be inspired by the songs of Hafiz to connect with who you truly were born to be. It is said that even Venus and the Messiah dance where the songs of Hafiz are sung. Who is the Messiah but the purity of the truth within you? Open your heart and allow for this coming. Long for it as you pick a card from this divine deck. I offer my life experience and the wisdom of my dearest friend and guide to assist you.

THE MYSTERY OF HAFIZ

It is true that love's ecstasy
has ruined my reputation,
but the essence of my existence
thrives on that ruin.

HAFIZ

VERY little is known about Hafiz as a person. All we can figure out about his life is through understanding his own words. Even that is not so reliable since his language is allegorical. We can only read what others have written about him to evaluate his writing style or comment on his background.

In fact, the compelling mystery of Hafiz is how elusive he can be when anyone tries to find the words to describe him: He vanishes before your eyes. His songs vanish on your tongue. You cannot pin him down and say, "This is what he does." It is best to read through his verses without stopping to analyze them. Read for the experience of what he is sharing with you. Read for the experience of coming to know this amazing Oracle.

Hafiz is as beautifully himself as anyone I have been involved with in my entire life; as an artist, a poet, a mystic, or whatever way you describe him. He is an artist in the sense of being a poet, but more importantly, Hafiz is a true artist in the sense of being himself. He is a wonderfully pure example of someone who has found a way of expressing divine words in a totally unique way. The understanding of his songs cannot be found in the manipulation of words. They are found in the heart — not the physical heart, or even the emotional heart. It is a quality of spirit that cannot be confined to a word.

Hafiz inspires us to go on a journey into a pure state and to become someone unique and true to ourselves as human beings. When we drown our minds in some way, we might discover the innocence in which we were created. This is a beautiful state of being. This is a phenomenon that the Oracle of Hafiz invites us to witness and experience.

Throughout his poetry, Hafiz guides us, charms us, whispers his secrets, and sees our beauty as human beings. He anoints us with the light of the moon, and he shares his presence, his laughter, his tears and his joy with us. These are all qualities that make us feel comfortable with him. This is what leads so many who read his poetry to see Hafiz as a real friend of the heart!

Lover and beloved, mystic and layman, Sufi and ascetic, hypocrite and libertine ... all relish the beautiful and soothing inspirations they discover in accordance with their own taste and apprehension. Everyone considers Hafiz to be their friend and guide once they know his work, no matter what values they uphold. This indicates the power of love that flows through this versatile Oracle.

Hafiz sees divine expression in every flower, even in the sleepy narcissus flower. He sees it in the enticing dance of the beauties in the garden, and in the golden beauty of the streaming rays of the sun. He writes of the alluring dance of the gypsy expressing her freedom around the fire beneath the moon.

An Oracle for Humankind

Hafiz lived during a dark period of history when the entire Middle East, India, and a major part of Russia were ruled by the vicious and bloodthirsty children of Genghis Khan. They were as horrible as their ancestors, teeming with rivalry and nepotism. In a situation like that, where freedom of speech was non-existent, Hafiz was forced to take his words to a level where the ordinary person would not understand their depth, so the meanings could always be changeable and defendable.

It is for this reason that the poetry of Hafiz often has a double meaning. At first glance, a single poem appears to speak of sensuous, secular matters. He talks of beautiful things on earth, such as nature and the beloved. But the exact same poem, when reflected on, bears an entirely spiritual meaning. It is this ability for abstraction that allowed Hafiz's work to flourish and stand out for its unusually multifaceted character. It is most interesting to observe the way his poetry speaks to anyone at any time in any place.

As an Oracle who knew the message around which the beginnings of freedom were shaped, Hafiz carefully builds into his poetry the path to freedom. He speaks through the symbolism of what people of his time felt was blasphemy. His deep humanity, using himself as the humble one with shortcomings, allowed him to slip into the glory of the God who was calling him to tell a new story for those around him.

The mission of Hafiz has been to give a more positive vision to the people, to give them hope, and to help restore their faith in themselves and each other. He considers physical beauty as a witness or a representation of divine beauty, and he uses this concept as his major expression.

To Hafiz, everything in this world has a beauty of its own, from the empty darkness to the fullness of the light, from that which people called 'bad' or 'evil' to the truth and grace of goodness. It is an evolving flow of transformation, a shift to creatively envision beauty as a welcome veil that blesses our existence.

Joy is a prayer that goes out in every direction, spreading the sweetness to every thirsty soul! Hafiz touches millions in this way. His words are filled with wine, with an open heart, with joy, with the presence of the beloved. He fills the cups of every soul!

There are not too many people in this world who can cross cultures like Hafiz. His message to humanity is this: Do not live without wine and love for even an instant. Every moment is the time for the blossoming of the roses. Every day is a new beginning.

Thousands of people visit the shrine of Hafiz every day as they go on a pilgrimage to pay tribute to this beautiful soul. Even more importantly, they are searching for themselves. Hafiz believes that love never dies. It is only the outer form we inhabit that dies. The spirit of love is the eternal spring of what is most pure in us. Love is the sparkling ruby beneath the dust on the path before the door of the beloved. Everyone will create their own tribute to the beauty discovered in the journey of their lives. This is the wisdom that Hafiz shares with us.

The Tongue of the Hidden

By those who have known him for centuries, the songs of Hafiz have been hailed as written by an Oracle. It is a tradition among the Persians to consult Hafiz when confronted with a difficult decision or choice. When they use the Divan of Hafiz as an Oracle, it is widely believed that his messages reveal the answer to our intent.

In almost every Iranian home, one can find a copy of the *Divan of Hafiz*. People use his poetry often as an entertaining ritual during gatherings. The group decides to ask him a certain question. Then they open the *Divan* randomly. The poem that opens usually offers guidance to each participant individually through the same poem. Every verse has inspired lines that seem to speak to all hearts in a way that answers each, assuring them of their own heart's longing. He is 'every man' in that sense, which is the vision of unity for all humankind.

What has led to this belief is that the songs of Hafiz are energized by an indescribable power that is nothing less than divine. They are enlightened by the divine connection that Hafiz has with the source of all existence. It is for this reason that Hafiz holds the title, 'The tongue of the hidden.' His songs reflect the language of the soul, which rises from the unconscious within us.

Hafiz is like a loving father who leads us to God, or someone who lifts a cup of light to our lips and offers us a drink to quench our thirst for truth. He has been called a beggar in the highest sense of the word. He lifts the state of being poor to mean innocence; a person without material things in life, or one without labels or fame. He is a true human being who doesn't need any attachment to be who he is.

Hafiz reaches for joy in his journey of sharing himself. He is positive, and he sees through the inner eyes of his heart. He shares what it means to be an artist of life. Everyone could perceive that differently, of course, but for Hafiz, it is a kindness, a loving gaze that sees the light of being a human soul.

He does not seem to invest in this world or in the next. He is engaged in the present moment in an absolutely beautiful way. He is such a divine Oracle that we are more and more attracted to be near him. One could say we fall in love, but not in the trivial sense of the word; it means to be full of care.

When someone is being true to who they are, they want the same for others. As a true Oracle, Hafiz leads us to clear away all that is false in us. If we have acquired attributes that are false, he offers us ways to purify ourselves. He shows us how to find the pearl within us, and the way to nurture and protect it to rediscover the luster of who we are.

As an alchemist, we reach for the gold. The sun is an image of this golden quality of light, and it pours its life-giving light upon everyone. It brings light to the darkness and mystery of our original nature. Hafiz sees this light in us and writes of its radiance. As an Oracle, he helps us to see who we truly are and how to be as radiant as the sun.

Using These Cards

Whenever you are facing a challenge, or you need to tap into divine wisdom for guidance, use this set of cards and the accompanying book to receive direction from Hafiz. By contemplating the song, along with its reflection and the inspired image, you are bound to receive some meaningful guidance. If you want to be guided, do not see this set of cards as divination or divine prophecy. Take them in as a directive for you to discover the truth of what it means to be yourself; to be true to being fully human.

    The best way to benefit from these cards is to contemplate clearly your dilemma before you pick a card. Picture yourself as one who is attuned to the source of a deeper wisdom. Close your eyes and visualize the vast beauty of infinity and the intimacy of the creative flow of existence. Now imagine the divine as an energy in the cards that wants to manifest in your life. Allow the love from the beautiful heart of Hafiz to open and clear the way. Then pick a card.

    First, read the song out loud several times, perhaps in a rhythmic way and meditate on it as you gaze deeper into the accompanying image. Do it in a similar way if you are reading in a group. Once you feel a loving presence that is centered in your intention, read the description in communion with your highest self. Let the living spirit of Hafiz open the way to find your heart and the beloved, and be ready to receive more detailed direction.

Allow Hafiz to come into your world as a creative power, filling your private sanctuary with energy and light. Open your heart and let him in to illuminate your life and anoint you with joy. What is offered to you is the key to being truly and uniquely yourself in the presence of *agape*, or the highest and purest love that one can experience. Reflect on the card as if you are receiving divine guidance that is only for you. Set your reasoning aside — surrender to the flow of the river of love that leads your dream toward the sea of delight. Await the fullness of each and every moment and live it fully now and with great joy!

May the spirit of Hafiz enlarge your own and seed the world around you with his wisdom of sweet madness.

CARD MESSAGES

SONG OF ABUNDANCE
Treasure is already within you.

*Don't complain about dearth,
for the fruits of life are
joy and sorrow, rose and thorn,
and ups and downs.*

HAFIZ

Life is not designed to be a smooth ride. There are ups and downs, joys and sorrows, positives and negatives that we have to face with grace. Yet, if we only focus on what is missing in our lives, we will be surrounding ourselves in unpleasant conditions. Through appreciating what is present to us, we will receive the kiss of life that offers us true joy and deeply intimate abundance.

Dearest! The spirit of Hafiz is drawing close to you to gentle your soul and steady your heart. Hafiz wants you to realize that you are capable of receiving the most precious treasure. A life of plenty is all love. Abundance is not a measure of life, but a thrilling way of living. Have courage and sacrifice your focus on selfish indulgence. Trust and accept what comes your way. Be appreciative of the spiritual and physical blessings that you are continuously receiving from the universe to tap into abundance. By having gratitude, you will allow the seeds of joy and happiness to germinate inside you into what you desire.

MANTRA
I am thankful for the abundant blessings that are fully present in my life.

SONG OF ASSURANCE
Follow your dream fearlessly.

*I am not one who is weak
against the turn of destiny.
I will undo the wheel of heaven
if it turns against my wish.*

HAFIZ

As a human being, you were born from a ray of divine glory. You are here to discover your life and create your own story. Your heart is the divine power and source of creating this assurance. Treasure what you harbor in your chest. Trust yourself and be assured that you are more capable than you think you are. Hafiz is a truly compassionate friend to guide you as an Oracle of wisdom and insight. Take the wheel of destiny in your hand, and alter its course to your deeper wisdom.

The spirit of Hafiz is challenging you not to feel weak against what you are unable to change. Use your strength and you will not fall short of your dreams. Fan the creative spark within you and feel how renewing it is to touch your innocence and purity. Have self-assurance and trust the flow of life. Envision new possibilities! Feel the rhythm of birthing new insight! Believe in yourself, and be content with the gift of who you are. Feel the assurance that nothing can dim the light that shines from within.

MANTRA
I will always overcome fear when actualizing what my heart kindles with creative vision!

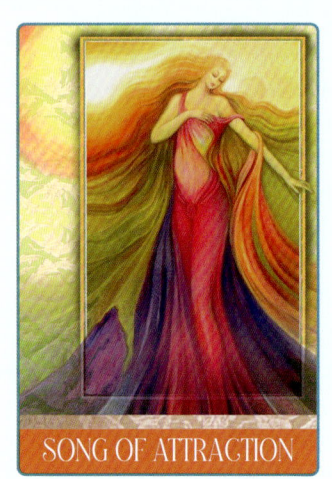

SONG OF ATTRACTION

Reflect the glory of love.

O Hafiz, stop drawing on the surface of water!
Mirror the splendor of love
and behold how you attract lovers!

HAFIZ

Capturing the hearts of people is a treasure that arouses pleasure. What attracts the heart is so much more than outer appearance. Just being a beautiful flower blowing in the wind won't create the energy that moves the heart. Hafiz is showing you the way to reflect the glory of love. He touches your heart and invites you to shine like the moon as it mirrors the divine light to illuminate the world.

Dearest! Don't be blind to your own attractive qualities. If you believe you are not enough, no matter how gorgeous you look, you'll always find something wrong, which will prevent your eyes from seeing your own beauty. Let the wine of love loosen your veil, and shine your merits brighter than the sun! Get drunk with beauty and fall in love with life! Dare to invite the thrill! Be your own source of positive emotions instead of requiring people or things to validate and complete you. Cultivate your confidence, spread more love and behold how you become more luminous to everyone.

MANTRA

I will reflect the light of love to let it radiate and vibrate through my true self!

SONG OF AWAKENING

Turn your dream into reality.

*Wake up and greet
the graceful beloved that appears
from behind the veil,
and hear your own cries of delight!*

HAFIZ

If you are experiencing a shift in your conscious awareness, you may be beginning a journey of spiritual awakening. This will be a wonderful transition! As your mindfulness expands, you will discover a part of you that has been lost or hidden among more mundane concerns. The mystery deepens and life takes on a special glow. You will feel more alive and inspired, and your daily life will thrive and become exciting in new ways.

Hafiz is awakening you to free the beloved that has been concealed inside of you. He is letting you know that you have the ability to effectively make the changes. Reach for the sources within that are waiting to turn your dreams into reality. Now is the time for you to embrace the beloved that is ready to manifest as love, harmony, and compassion in your life. Know that you are endowed with the power that you need to face the challenges that come your way. Be gentle with yourself and trust the higher power flowing through you.

MANTRA
I will become more aware and move toward awakening the beloved within myself.

SONG OF BEAUTY
Behold through the eyes of love.

*Gaze at the graceful face of the beloved
to learn the love of beauty,
for the real joy in life is to be consumed
by loveliness.*

HAFIZ

You are born to enjoy this life in an infinite variety of ways. The key to joy is to experience the essence of beauty and the presence of love in whatever you face in life. The more beauty you behold, the more you are transformed. You discover true joy! When you focus your attention on seeing beauty, the thrill of the journey invites you to become a lover. Steer clear of making judgments, and you will feel happy and at peace. Immerse yourself in beauty.

Hafiz is an amazing Oracle, softening and opening you like a gentle guide to love. Look for beauty around you, and make this your natural way of seeing. When you use your imagination and fill yourself with beauty, you will discover you have been consumed by loveliness. You will begin to notice that everything around you has a beauty of its own. You experience what it means to be not only a lover of people you meet but also a lover of nature. You learn to appreciate the beauty of a bird flying above your head, or a tiny flower that has grown in the crack of the asphalt. This is a way of being that shoots you like an arrow in the direction of a beloved that will exalt your life. You begin to live as love, as being in love, and slowly and deliciously you'll dissolve into love.

MANTRA
I am committing myself to look for the beauty in everything that I face in life.

SONG OF CELEBRATION

Live life as a blessing.

*If I am drunk on the night of fasting,
don't condemn me.
The beloved was endearingly kind,
and a jug of wine was at my bedside.*

HAFIZ

There are challenges in life that we live into day by day and moment by moment. If we are forced to face them as obligations, we lose the joy. But if we see our daily work as a true expression and manifestation of life, we can find ways to meet each day as a celebration.

Hafiz is offering you the chance to see life as an invitation. You are in this world to enjoy every moment. There are no wrong turns; every adventure and misadventure is part of the journey.

When resources and possibilities for enjoyment are available, why would anyone set aside the opportunity for an unknown future? Take every occasion to celebrate life as a gift! Even a small achievement can be joyful. The more you focus on life as a blessing, the more likely you are to feel the generosity and benevolence of the universe. Use your abilities and learn to develop and nurture them to transform your day. Consider your life as a garden and create beauty wherever you are, planting seeds of love to inspire you and those around you. You have the power to completely transform how you feel about your life, and how you spend your time here on Earth in every moment.

MANTRA
Today, I'm celebrating my life, my power, and the joy of living.

SONG OF CHALLENGE
Follow your passion with confidence.

*A true lover always catches
the attention of the beloved.
Pain is what we need;
remedy is endless.*

HAFIZ

You have been created with a joy that lifts you beyond your limitations. Don't hold back because it's unknown to you. Listen to the song of Hafiz that streams from his compassion and pure love. He is kindly telling you that if you want to embrace success, accept that pain and struggle are a part of life. There is potential at the heart of every challenge. Endure and you are sure to move toward an exciting reward.

Dearest! You are empowered by a passionate energy to pursue the desire and commandment of your heart above all else. A true lover is bold, truthful, and unafraid of failure. Open your heart to the gift of faith and trust in divine protection! Awaken to the presence of divine kindness and generosity and move fearlessly into dangerous waters! Be courageous and disappear into the light of love, the way the moon and the stars disappear into the rising sun. Let the power of love cover you in an armor of light and set you free to go anywhere, to be anything, and to face whatever comes along. This is the secret song of your precious heart!

MANTRA

I am open to receiving new energy from the divine presence to face my life's challenges.

SONG OF CHANGE

Create your life to reflect your desire.

Don't bind my heart like a bale of hay,
let me hold
the tip of your hair to unravel my confusion
and find the way.

HAFIZ

When life seems to be drained of all purpose and reason, it is time to create a new season to inspire. Access your divine gift of imagination and use it to attract new opportunities. When you are in the playground of creativity, you'll draw on your own abilities and what is natural for you.

Hafiz comes as a spiritual essence that surrounds and shelters you with pure love. He has come to help you take the first step toward whatever it is that you long to achieve. When you follow a strand of your beloved's hair, it will eventually lead you to the face of the beloved. Every step you take along this path is a clue that reveals a new reality. Be confident that change will bring great satisfaction for you. Try not to judge change as a negative, because you never know what possibilities might open to you. Be free from obsessive concerns and know that you are starting on a new path that is more suited to you — and perhaps more exciting!

MANTRA
I commit to recreating my life to reflect my desire to live authentically.

SONG OF COMMUNION

Find the power of intimacy in love.

*From the dawning of eternity
to the dusk of infinite darkness,
the flowering bond of friendship
blooms from promises of love.*

HAFIZ

Love is truly the power that helps to unite living beings to complete and fulfill them. Communion takes place when we utilize the resources that are deep within us. The lover is transformed in the beloved and the beloved in the lover. An aura surrounds the lovers when their gazes fall upon one another.

The spirit of Hafiz is singing in your heart and cells to draw others to you through the power of love. He is creating ways for you to express the wonder of becoming a being of love and joy. Let your friendship grow into the communion that could lead to pure love. The way to achieve this is to begin making changes to allow love to flow through you. Enlarge your view by sharing this wonderful feeling of abundance and joy with everyone. When you are in the intimacy of love, your longing inspires more love and moves the creativity and power within you.

MANTRA
I am open to the rising energy of love and to the gift of feeling the beloved everywhere.

SONG OF COURAGE
Defend your heart's desire with conviction.

*The kingdom of courage and contentment
is a treasure
that even the sultan cannot capture
with a sword.*

HAFIZ

You were born with the capacity to catch a great vision for your life and bring that vision to fruition. When you ride the steed of courage with conviction, the world around you moves in to support you. As you travel forward, you will feel like you are guided by some mysterious power. Your confidence and courage expand when you take command. The door of new beginnings opens, and invites and excites you to enter into a new way of life.

Hafiz is coming to you in spirit as a support and encouragement to help you grow into a greater awareness of the wonder of who you are. Don't allow fear to keep you from taking the leap to find the golden path meant for you! Let your life become a new adventure! When you take action and courage guides your choices, you will flourish and ride fearlessly into your future. Be bold and let the vision that is seeking to express itself manifest as the best reflection of who you truly are. Face the challenges before you with confidence and grace; you have the leadership ability within you. Your birthright is just waiting for you to discover it! Cultivate and express your vibrant potential and feel the energy it generates.

MANTRA
I will venture forward fearlessly, riding on my strength in the service of my vision.

SONG OF CREATION
You are formed to bloom.

*Plant the tree of love,
for it bears the fruit that feeds the heart.
Uproot the hostile sapling,
for it brings suffering to the soul.*

HAFIZ

Inside your heart, there is a garden of life constantly growing and developing. This garden is your spirit. Love radiates the light of joy upon this spiritual garden in much the same way as the sun shines on a physical garden. When the garden of your heart is brightened with true love, you will feel an unlimited power and an ever-expanding creative energy within yourself.

Dearest! Have the assurance that the love of the creator and the power to create is already embedded within you. The song of Hafiz is an invitation to let the seeds of love germinate and sprout inside your heart. When your soul is filled with joy, the essence of creativity begins to manifest. It blooms into a natural flowering and expansion of unlimited creative expression! You have been given the tools and the power to cultivate your uniqueness. Empty yourself and become free from your assumptions, expectations, fears, and prejudices. Take this opportunity to become the best version of yourself. Use your inner creative potential, and open the portal between the imaginal and mundane worlds to live fully and creatively.

MANTRA

I am going to design my own life by using the great creative power within me.

SONG OF DESIRE
Kindle your desire for life.

The bud of your desire will blossom when you serve it lovingly, like the breeze caressing dawn.

HAFIZ

Desire is the spark that fuels inspiration. It is the starting point of all achievement and transformation. Desire leads you to turn away from negative thoughts and follow your inner wisdom. You can create your desired life by accepting what is not in your control and modifying what you are able to change.

Hafiz is the mystical friend who is showing you the secret path toward what you truly desire, what you most want to see, or what you long to feel. You are guided and supported by the divine Spirit to serve your highest desire sweetly and tenderly. If you're looking to be happy in your personal life or cultivate a deeper meaning in your relationships, you need to risk being more courageous and brave! Have faith in your own abilities. Don't be concerned with what others might think or say. Find your own exciting way! You are the only person in charge of your own wellbeing. Your guideline is already placed within your own heart. Listen to it and do your part to follow the flow of grace. Soon, you'll discover that you have found what you once thought was beyond your reach. The desires of pure love touch the spires of heaven.

MANTRA
I am letting go of my negative thoughts to realize the joy of my happiness.

SONG OF DETERMINATION

Move forward; trusting divine guidance.

The sweet success I was hoping to find
in my fortune
was hidden in the curls of the beloved's hair.

HAFIZ

When the going becomes difficult, we call on our power of perseverance and determination. No matter how hard it is, or how long it takes, being steadfast will be your driving power. Hafiz showers you with light and holds out his hand to say, "Come, I will guide you on the way that leads you to the beloved." Accept the ups and downs of life, and follow the path of your dream with joy and determination. Perseverance turns the journey into sweet vintage wine.

Dearest! Let the songs of Hafiz lift your soul. Pursue the divine music that feels especially meaningful to you and moves your heart. Have the confidence that you are being guided in every pursuit of life you seek. As you faithfully follow your longings, new ways will open, and you will be swept into the flow and feel blessings beyond your dreams. Feel the compassionate energy of Hafiz — surrender and trust in his wisdom. Be determined, and continue along the path of love into the arms of your destiny.

MANTRA
I'm determined to follow the direction of my love through the ups and downs of life.

SONG OF DREAMS
Dance to the music of your desire.

*Longing for the wine of love
burned all my belongings the day I saw
the image of the wine giver
in the shimmering flames of the wine.*

HAFIZ

Some people live in a dream world; some face reality. The truly successful people are those who turn their dreams into reality. The fear of failure and the loss of desire to continue are often what steal the wonder of achieving dreams. Hafiz speaks to you in the mystery from the corner of the wine house to offer you a cup of dreams. Quiet your thoughts and listen to your heart. Let the music of desire guide you to manifest your longings. Allow the wine of love to help you create from your heart and you will live the beauty of your dreams.

Dearest, you have within you the strength, the patience, and the passion to reach for the stars to change the world. Dream no small dreams for they have no power to move the heart. Follow your dream toward the life you have imagined for yourself, and open your arms to confidently embrace success. The only person who can stop you from fulfilling your aspirations is you; to accomplish great things, you must dream, have faith, and act on it. Always be vigilant for ways to nurture and inspire your dreaming.

MANTRA
I am letting my heart reveal and guide my most precious dreams.

SONG OF FAITH
You have the key to open any lock.

*Every sorrow becomes a joyful relief
for the seeker
who remains faithful in the promise
of safekeeping.*

HAFIZ

Feeling positive about your ability to face challenges can make your life blissful. The power that drives this lies in the faith that you can find creative solutions to handle pressures that come your way. Without faith, you may fall short of your hopes and dreams and begin to doubt your ability to bring them into expression. The oracle is awakening your heart to develop a divine trust to face challenges head-on.

The spirit of Hafiz is entering the garden of your dreams to sow the seed that will sprout into the tree of triumph. He has come to nourish your soul by helping you to fulfill your calling. The seed of success lies in your inborn ability; have faith in yourself to face challenges along the way. Open the portal to major breakthroughs and leave nothing to chance. If you are always in relationship with the truth of who you truly are, your faith will never diminish. Success comes by not allowing setbacks to keep you down. Follow your dreams with devotion, and trust the power that guides you in the creative process.

MANTRA
I have faith in my own ability to face whatever challenges come my way.

SONG OF FLOW
Surrender to the river of life.

*Neither Noah's life remains,
nor the kingdom of Alexander.
Be a dervish; keep moving in the flow
to create something new!*

HAFIZ

Nothing is permanent in this unpredictable world. Why carry past memories or dreams of the future to limit your life's journey? Why not meet challenges as an opportunity to create new dreams? Walk with Hafiz! Be inspired by this gracious and loving Oracle — he will guide you with humor and imagination. Listen to your own flowering heart's desire and follow it faithfully.

O dear one! Your human nature is aligned with the rhythm and kindness of the divine creator; trust it! Your life only truly exists and is unfolding in the present moment. Your desire is connected with deep insight that flows in your soul like a light in the universe. You carry the seeds of the divine! This is a calling! Have the faith to explore, envision, and create exciting new pathways in your life. Discover the patience to playfully stay in the flow. Let the 'friend' of Hafiz intimately guide you to know the hour of God. Stay in the flow and surrender to this creative power within that you could never have imagined before.

MANTRA

I am going to live every day as if I am experiencing life for the very first time.

SONG OF FORGIVENESS

Clear the darkness from your soul.

*A voice shouted from the corner
of the wine house last night:
There is a pleasure in forgiveness
that can't be found in revenge!*

HAFIZ

When you are hurt by someone, it is natural to react and to dwell on what happened. But it takes up more space if you hold on too long. The *Song of Forgiveness* is about releasing your initial hostility and forgiving the person who caused this pain. Let go of any feelings of revenge or wanting to get even.

The spirit of Hafiz has come with divine wisdom to guide you. Embrace his compassionate invitation with grace and love! Free your soul and move on. Settle any disagreement and know you can't change what happened in the past. Dearest! Draw on the love within you. We all make mistakes, and forgiveness softens the hurt and sets you free. Don't be a person who is identified by carrying resentment or holding a grudge. Choose peace, and you will make room for love and joy.

MANTRA
I will let go of the pain of past and focus on the grace of moments of love and joy.

SONG OF FREEDOM
You were born to be free.

*How can I soar to the height of freedom
when I'm burdened
by the weight of my material attachments
and toil?*

HAFIZ

Hafiz is anointing you with his enchanting insight. This gentle Oracle shines his light to show you the presence of divine help in so many forms in your life. Your time in this world is too precious to spend it all in the service of personal attachments and material wants. You were born to be free, and with the ability to pursue your own lifestyle and plan your future. The only one who can truly limit your freedom is you.

You are invited by Hafiz to live into your liberation and allow freedom to bring you the light of illumination. The Oracle has come to help you create a new world by witnessing the protection hidden in the mystery of existence. You can truly be free when you are willing to deliver yourself from the limitations and restrictions imposed by your own thoughts and actions. With the power of your heart, expand your life by realizing and expressing your capabilities to achieve any dreams you've cast aside. Stand firm in the present moment of your own human spirit to truly live your freedom.

MANTRA
I free myself from the attachments that hold me captive to my selfish wants and habits.

SONG OF FRIENDSHIP
Welcome the purity of the kindred spirit.

*I regret and grieve
that I didn't know until now
the alchemy of success
is friendship, my friend.*

HAFIZ

Everyone longs for a loving connection with others. Friendship is what brings purpose and meaning to our lives and offers joy to our soul. Hafiz sees friendship as the means for having a successful life. Through sharing his own personal experience, he emphasizes the acute value of robust friendships and a healthy social life. Spreading the scent of love is the essence with which you can enjoy communion.

Beloved, the wine of love and friendship is a greater blessing than you might ever realize. Friendship heightens the quality of your life, creates an alchemy of great energy, and anoints you with joy. By pursuing your passion, you will have the opportunity to meet caring friends whose support you'll enjoy. When you do things with others, you will not only have their support, but you will receive unexpected help from the world around you. The impossible becomes possible as you align yourself with others. Trust that divine flow will lead you to meet the purity of the kindred spirit who comes as a friend.

MANTRA
I will seek to discover the kind of love that can help me be a better friend to others.

SONG OF GRATITUDE
Take everything as a gift of grace.

*Whatever is poured in the vessel,
we gratefully drink.
Be it nectar from heaven,
or simply this earthly wine.*

HAFIZ

Sometimes, we become so busy with details that we forget to attend to those who are so valuable in our lives. Through the wisdom of his insight, Hafiz is the Oracle who has come to reveal the way for you to show gratitude. When you appreciate others and focus on your gratitude, you allow disappointments to fade away and love to appear. This is the way to turn our everyday moments into works of pure joy.

Hafiz is awakening you through the generosity of his presence and wisdom. Transform the ordinary into a gift of grace through practicing trust and thankfulness. Let gratitude become a foundation for your life, and behold how miracles begin to appear all around you along the way. When you embrace with appreciation what you have, you will feel that you have more than before and you create your own grace. From then on, gratitude becomes your attitude, and you will flower into friendships that will enrich your life.

MANTRA
I will open my heart to behold and be grateful for what I have around me.

SONG OF GUIDANCE
Look for the clues to success.

*When words flow from the heart,
don't label them "wrong".
You are missing the gist, my dear.
This is what is wrong.*

HAFIZ

Divine guidance is being offered to you by Hafiz to enrich your connection to the world around you. This guidance is coming your way to remove the uncertainty that could be holding you back from your full potential. You are enriched with the presence of divine help that shows up in so many ways. The Oracle helps to open the portal of your own vision and understanding.

The spirit of Hafiz caresses and surrounds you with care, showering you with the light of vision. Hafiz sings to you and becomes your sweet guide. He holds out his hand to say, "Come, I will be with you. Let me walk with you into a new way of being." Have faith and feel the guidance and compassion of those who have walked the path before you. Be open to discovering ways to make your life richer and fuller. Feel the help and support of Hafiz as a friend and have the courage to make these changes. Honest and sincere guidance that you can trust is what can bring you wholeness. It inspires you to grow, to gain new insight, and to further develop your character.

MANTRA

I am open and willing to receive guidance that comes from the heart of those who have walked the path.

SONG OF HAPPINESS

Experience the joy of spreading love.

*There are infinite reasons in this world
for us to be happy.
All those reasons are rooted in the potential
for love.*

HAFIZ

When we look into the lives of happy people, we discover their happiness is the result of having love in their heart. Hafiz defines happiness as the perfume of the rose of love, the light shining from the candle of love, and the whisper from the sound of love. He is calling the child within you to come out and play. He wants you to release the idea of perfection and take every opportunity to see the fun side of life. When happiness evolves from love, there is no limit to the satisfaction of the appetite.

Dear one! The world around you is full of prospects for lighthearted pursuits. Live a less-guarded life, and get involved with the activities you love! Open the door to allow your creative juices to flow and use your God-given gift of creativity with full confidence. You don't have to chase extraordinary moments to find happiness. Be open to giving and receiving love and be willing to sacrifice to improve the quality of your life. Let the sweetness of your longings guide you.

MANTRA
I feel love for everything inside me and intend to spread it around like the scent of roses.

SONG OF HARMONY
Align your body and soul in unity.

*Whether I am a rose or a thorn,
there is a vigilant florist arranging me
in the bouquet of this life
so tenderly with his loving hands.*

HAFIZ

Life is too valuable to waste on worrying. To spend it well is to live in harmony. Blend the flow of your body, mind, and heart together, and let your spirit sing. You can achieve inner peace when there is no conflict or competition with your corporeal elements. Keep your body and your soul in harmony. When you focus too much on one and neglect the other, life falls out of balance.

When love blossoms in your heart, it offers the grace that moves your body and soul toward unity. Spend time with friends, wander in nature, get better sleep, and expand your quiet time. Trust that joy is always headed your way, and that more enthusiasm and confidence will fortify your belief. Your mind will find clarity, your memory will expand, and your vision will increase to achieve your goals. Your life improves and your soul achieves more peace.

MANTRA
I will balance and harmonize my life by aligning with my natural flow of love and peace.

SONG OF HONESTY
Honor the truth of what you are.

*Seekers of truth
don't trade even a grain of barley
for the lavish robe of those
whose virtue is only a pose.*

HAFIZ

Greatness in an individual is empowered by honesty. It calls you to be real and true to yourself. Hafiz is the brave soul who paves the way to guide you! He is the Oracle of truth, and is both humble and compassionate. He is inspiring you to do things not just to be praised, but to be strong enough to live your truth. He wants you to develop honor in how you solve problems and find solutions. Search your heart for a kind response! This helps you grow toward the expression of your best self.

Hafiz urges you to discover your own power and gifts. Realize your uniqueness and use it! Be anointed in the wine of love and drop the disguises to impress others. No need to wear a false robe when you stand tall and true to all! When you do not deceive, you receive the inspiration you need; then you will see and feel what it means to be free!

MANTRA
I am determined to faithfully follow my heart and find my way to true honesty.

SONG OF HOPE
Achieve success through divine grace.

*If the wheel of fortune
does not spin in your favor for a day or so,
its setting will not always remain the same;
don't grieve!*

HAFIZ

There are moments of difficulty in life when we truly need help. Hope is the power that helps us break through the challenges. It can build our confidence to find our way even in the midst of misfortune. Hope is the divine grace that can conquer our fears, dry our tears, and light our way to the life we want.

    Hafiz is a friend of the heart who whispers an intimate message of hope and encouragement in your ear. He has come to illuminate your vision and lead you through the darkness and fear that may arise with uncertainty. Let yourself be lifted to a place beyond the burdens that you feel, and you will realize a love within you that is seeking your freedom. Surrounded by the glow, you are drawn into a community of friends who welcome you into the light of a greater sun. All is as it is meant to be. Soon you will be shifting from hope to a realization of the spiritual goals closest to your heart.

MANTRA

I am determined to pursue and achieve the vision for my ideal life, and have faith that I can accomplish it.

SONG OF HUMILITY
Release the ego to express your kindness.

I can no longer hide myself under a robe of arrogance. It is time for me to dance and live the life of a dervish.

HAFIZ

Hafiz has come as a friend and an Oracle to share a secret revelation. Surrender the covering of the ego; instead, take on the robe of a dervish and be humble. Awaken to the gift of grace that is within you as divine energy. Let humility move you into the source of who you are. Release the ego and guide what flows through you to express your 'one-of-a-kindness.' Embrace the beauty of your heart by allowing love to find a voice within you. Feel the bliss lifting your spirit as it rises on spread wings, and hear how it sings for thee when you are free.

Dearest! Don't allow your desire to become great and well-known to distance you from those you love. This would be a lonely road. Welcome the flight and the sweet tones and shadows of the night to transform you. Prepare yourself to be kissed by the light in the morning mist. When the ego becomes small beneath the moon and sky, then the heart can truly fly!

MANTRA
I will let my heart guide my life toward love and honor!

SONG OF INTIMACY
Seek tenderness from those with open hearts.

*I've been looking for a friend
whose bountiful presence
would sweeten my heart
and inspire a flood of desire.*

HAFIZ

You have come into this world as an exceptional part of the universe. You are a unique piece of the puzzle of humanity. Your nature is developed by a longing for intimate relationships that appear in various ways throughout your life. Your peace of mind comes when you develop a sense of communion with others and realize what you can share with them.

The flowing spirit of Hafiz is singing to you from beyond this existence. He wishes to inspire you to keep company only with those who can sweeten your heart, whose presence brings out your best. The Oracle is guiding you to let the quality of your close relationships give your life its deep meaning. Achieve intimacy through taking every step that could lead to emotional closeness. Trust the universe to give you what is your fair due. Wait in faith for the person who will appreciate and freely want what you have to give and they will come to you. Use the gift of love to create a truly heartfelt relationship. Focus not on what others do, but on keeping to your own higher purpose. You can always touch a friend's heart by expressing yourself sweetly, fully, honestly, and vulnerably.

MANTRA
I am going to strengthen my intimate relationships through presenting and expressing more love.

SONG OF JOY

Your soul is here to experience joy.

*If reason were aware
what joy the heart feels in the snare
of the beloved's hair, even the wise would be
enchained in madness!*

HAFIZ

Joy is a penetrating energy that loosens the bonds holding us captive to our attachments. When the heart is filled with music and songs of joy, there is no space for thoughts of worry to enter the mind. You have been created to enjoy life and follow your heart's desire. The ability to love what you have or give it away is in your hands.

   Dearest! Hafiz is showing you the way to open yourself to the healing shower of delight. True joy comes to you when you are caught in the beloved's hair. This is truly a path to walk with pleasure, for it indeed leads to your fulfillment. When you do everything with love, you are flowing with joy. Pure love lies within you as a gift and a grace to awaken you to your essence. Love always lures you toward the creative play and journeying of spirit. You are encouraged to concentrate on living in the now and dreaming about the future. This is how you stir up excitement for whatever it is that you are longing for in your life.

MANTRA
I am taking intentional action to be fully present to life, and to enjoy the journey every day.

SONG OF LEISURE
Take time out to renew yourself.

*I struggled and suffered for forty years,
never knowing
the remedy I was seeking
was in a jug of wine.*

HAFIZ

Everything that we do in life is a prelude to attaining love and ecstasy. When we spend our time simply enduring routine tasks, we lose motivation. A seducer is needed to inspire us to play and take time out to have some fun! The song of Hafiz invites you to let go of the brawl for a while and taste the wine of freedom. When you spend too much time thinking and worrying and feeling the pressures of life, you lose your capacity for joy. Let your heart guide you.

The spirit of Hafiz is here to hold your hand and lead you along the path of your dream. Let him lift your spirit to a place beyond the burdens you feel. Hafiz wants you to be like the flowers that gently lay back their petals and release a fragrance to sweeten our lives. Listen to a running brook nearby and rest a while in the cool grass among the violets. Let your body go quiet and wait for your spirit to rise freely — experience the truth for yourself. Feel the lightness of your own being. Flow with the loving kindness and generosity of the breath of the Divine. Balance your life between work and leisure. Turn what you have to do into what you love to do.

MANTRA
I will give my rational mind a break and remember my capacity to enjoy life.

SONG OF LIFE

Imbue your life with blissful moments.

*One who does not plant a seed of love,
or pick a rose of kindness,
is like a sentry hovering over tulips
in the wayward path of the wind.*

HAFIZ

Life is a song we sing and the love we share. No one ever truly knows all there is to understand about designing a life and bringing it into being. We live into the challenge day by day and moment by moment. Everything that we do opens infinite possibilities for us to respond creatively. We strive to find joy in the pleasures that come along. We draw on faith to use our ability to face the unexpected. This is our song of life.

Hafiz is a beacon of light pointing the way to help you develop and nurture your talents. He is showing you how to design your life as a healing and loving power. There are many more ways to enjoy life besides just being the custodian of the warehouse of our belongings. Create your life as a pilgrimage of your soul, moving like a particle toward the light. Use your unique ability to spread love and kindness. When you utilize qualities of perseverance, reliability, patience, and loyalty, you'll be able to create a life that is the best that it can be. This way, you will make your life more fun, more creative, and you will always be discovering something new as you move forward. Let your life be a song of love.

MANTRA

I am crafting my life with an open heart, a peaceful soul, and a creative spirit.

SONG OF LONGING
Enhance the fire of love
through yearning.

*Those who let longing be the driver
in their journey of life
will not feel the pain of separation.*

HAFIZ

When we lose our peace, it can happen for so many reasons. We need to seek the source within us to find a solution. Hafiz comes to you as an Oracle to share that your deepest longing of the heart is for love. He encourages you to move more toward something that you love so your soul will be filled with light and joy. Feel free to express love and be open enough to receive it.

The fire of love expands with longing! Allow this passionate energy to flow from your heart and reach for your beloved. When your desire becomes the lantern, you will reach your wholeness. Listen to Hafiz and let longing blaze in your heart, creating a fire that will guide you to feel the essence of joy. Fall into the energy of longing for love to be reborn in the renaissance of your own awakening! When love is flowing, you will find healing for your soul and peace will land in your heart.

MANTRA
I am letting the impulse of longing enrich my life.

SONG OF LOVE
Let your heart lead the way.

*Even if the urn is from heaven,
pour it out,
for the sweetest wine
is bitter without love.*

HAFIZ

The radiant light of Hafiz's mystical wisdom is coming your way, cascading as an outpouring of love to illuminate your inner world. Close your eyes for a moment and feel the presence of this gentle Oracle. Breathe the musky scent of love from the heart of Hafiz as it spreads to deliver a message to your heart. Let the wine of love free your thoughts. Silence your logical mind, and allow love to awaken your heart to the freedom of pure joy!

O dear one! Open your being to the healing nectar from the light of love! Accept it as an offering of grace pouring from a great and loving heart. This is the generous Source from which you come. This is a love that truly seeks your freedom. Release your ego, and set your judgment aside. See the world through the vision of an Oracle who has come to guide you as a friend. Let the feeling of love soothe your soul and change the way you view the world. Grow into maturity and the beauty of loving, and bloom into the discovery of your creative life. This loving gift is both your heritage and your destiny.

MANTRA

I will allow love to quiet my mind and bring joy to everything I do in life.

SONG OF NATURE

Rest in the comforting arms of spring.

*The garden and the meadow
are alive with the breath of spring!
Let us savor the flowing stream,
for all else is an elusive dream!*

HAFIZ

Hafiz is touching your heart, inviting you to bask in nature and behold the breath of spring. He wants to hold your hand and stroll in the garden. Listen to his songs telling you about the loveliness of light and the value of shadow. Allow the heart that has been singing love songs for hundreds of years to offer this pure and genuine quality to your life.

Hafiz is tenderly offering you the elixir that cures doubt and lack of vision. Follow the remedy of this gentle Oracle to increase your vision and discover a renewed energy of focus and vitality. If you feel you have worked hard to nourish other people and projects, it is now time to connect your inner source with nature. This is how you can acquire a marvelous clarity to face your challenges creatively. Let the energy of nature seed its alchemy within you to enrich the flow of your life. Rest in nature's comforting arms and feel its fragrance sweeten your wandering like the night-blooming jasmine.

MANTRA
I will spend more time in nature to awaken my capacity for sensing beauty.

SONG OF OPTIMISM
Be positive and live your dream.

*Look for the hidden jewel of compassion,
not causes for guilt;
only those with no ability
attempt to find faults.*

HAFIZ

This song reveals to you the way to transform negative thoughts with divine vision. Hafiz is appearing to help you see things with a constructive mindset, and change your attitude in a highly creative way. With a positive approach, you can see challenges as opportunities that help you follow your dream with confidence. Use an optimistic attitude as a vessel that can move you joyfully through life.

Dearest! It is true that beauty attracts attention, but having a positive attitude is what captures the heart. Respond with a unique and innovative expression to the invitation. Behold how you can inspire and excite a flow of oneness. A new experience is hidden in the heart of every challenge. Trust your intuition to guide you toward the right action and direction. Believe you can keep moving forward in the flow — new opportunities for joy and delight will appear before you and light your way.

MANTRA
I will use my imagination to transform the flow of energy toward living my dream.

SONG OF PERSEVERANCE

Surrender your doubts to find the path.

*True that the beloved's heart
is not won through efforts alone;
O heart! Better to strive to make
your highest endeavor known.*

HAFIZ

True joy in life comes to those who move in the flow toward reaching their dream. Tasting the pleasure of being in the beloved's arms can be achieved through persistent longing and deep attraction. Hafiz is a tender Oracle who comes to you as a true guide to support the secrets of your heart. He is a spirit, a poet, a mystic who has powerfully moved with persistence his whole life, and continues with deep wisdom in a timeless existence.

Dearest, you've been gifted with the ability to respond to all that happens around and within you. This is a beautiful revelation as you face your challenges. Listen to the Oracle whispering to you and let your perseverance be the driving force along the path of your dreams. Surrender your doubts and fears within you and behold how you will be anointed with imaginative ideas. No matter how intimidating or difficult a situation may seem, you have what it takes to move through it successfully. Do not give up. Open yourself to new and innovative approaches and trust you will instinctively find a way to successfully achieve your dreams in your lifetime.

MANTRA
I'm determined to live my life with patience and trust.

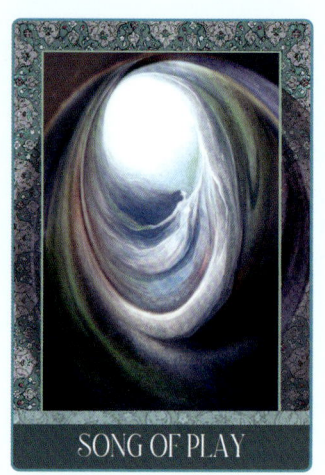

SONG OF PLAY

Gift your inner child fun and joy.

*If the string holding my prayer beads
broke apart, accept my excuse.
My hand was touching the skirt of the wine
giver's silvery thighs.*

HAFIZ

Playfulness is a light that illuminates our inner world and leads us toward love and ecstasy. Any time we overindulge ourselves in seriousness, we are welcoming the potential for frustration. Hafiz is inviting you to give more time to playfulness, even in the midst of solicitous endeavors. He is guiding you to reach for your inner child and make time for fun, for when there is laughter in love, there is always an afterglow. Be in love with life, whatever you are doing.

Dearest! You are capable of creating anything within your ability by focusing on it with purity of intent. Don't let your daily work or life routines consume all your time in a way that would cause you to burn out. Love is calling to increase your sense of wellbeing, and wants to augment your kindness and caring. Make time each day to dance and play. It's never a mistake to hold life's moments precious, and find some time for fun and joy. Let love enhance your faith and give you stamina and personal power. Allow your heart to lead the way on this journey of life, for love is truly a sacred play.

MANTRA
*I will find time to play, time for fun,
and time for love.*

SONG OF POWER
Awaken to the divinity within you.

*The universe could not bear
the burden of divine trust;
they cast a lot in heaven and my name,
the jester, was drawn.*

HAFIZ

This is a sacred hour to awaken! You hold a power inside that is far greater than you realize. It is waiting for you to claim it as your own. The key to unlocking this power is your belief that you truly have it. Hafiz is whispering a secret to you from his gentle heart — he calls you out to realize that the divine wine is yours. He will guide you to use this gift to create more of what you long for in life.

Dearest! Open your heart and awaken to the divinity within you. Reach for the powerful qualities that have been embedded in your essence. Feel the presence! Let the divine gift that you have help you to fully activate your mission and purpose. Don't allow anxiety, regret, loneliness, or anger to keep you from benefitting from this great power. Instead, focus on your grace. Embrace this treasure and allow it to gently guide you into your rightful place. When you truly align with all that you long for, the energy will lead you along the right path. Soon, you will be shining as you were born to do.

MANTRA
I will harness my inner power and direct it toward my purpose for the benefit of all.

SONG OF PRESENCE
Be aware of every moment.

*Treasure your time
as long as you can.
Life is only this moment;
be aware, my dear.*

HAFIZ

Moments in life seem so brief that we are barely mindful of them as they pass. Our response can initiate difficult consequences if we are not committed to consciously seeking a quality life. The compassionate guidance of Hafiz is reminding you not to dwell on the past or worry about the future. Be fully present to what is happening. Trust your heart and listen to it.

Dearest! You were born and created out of the greatness of the Source of All Life. You can receive revelations of kindness in a moment of mindfulness. It comes to you when you see with clarity of vision through the eyes of love. Liberation is to let your heart sing and open your wings! Who knows what will happen next? Trust that your life is guided. Every hour can offer you a variety of satisfying experiences, so welcome the treasure of unexpected pleasures! Realize they may never come again. Embrace life and experience every moment fully. Let grace guide the way you live with yourself and others.

MANTRA

I'm determined to stay aware and be present to the opportunities for success in my life.

SONG OF REBIRTH
Recreate yourself as the hero
of your dream.

*When the breeze scatters
the scent of love,
even a lifeless heart
becomes fully alive.*

HAFIZ

Hafiz is approaching you with divine revelation. He wants you to set sail for a new horizon and give birth to your dream. He has come as soft as the breeze to help you blow away your familiar routines, stagnant situations, or challenging relationships that no longer support or empower you.

Dearest! You were born with the capacity to cultivate a great vision for your life. You are destined to live your dream because the guiding light is within you. Seek inside your heart to find the love that wants to be you. Now is the time to focus on revealing yourself. The world is waiting for you to emerge. Move some energy around. Use your power! Visualize how you want to express the fullness and completeness of who you truly are! Take the first step, and see how you will be miraculously guided toward the next. As you move forward, any doubt that usually pauses your actions will move aside, and your confidence and courage will increase.

MANTRA
I give birth to a new 'me' who can boldly face any challenges.

SONG OF RELIEF

Change your belief; allow time for relief.

*A dervish who has nothing has no worry.
Planning and contemplation
are for the committed ones.*

HAFIZ

If the world is feeling too heavy, and your burdens are more than you can bear, it's time to make a change. When your mind is caught in the waves and whirls of old programming, you can lose your sense of creativity. Hafiz is inviting you to transform the feeling of being liable into having the control. Wake up with a smile. Be more playful and remember joy!

Love has many dimensions and there are so many ways to love! Being too serious and thinking too much can deplete your energy. Hafiz calls you to the wisdom of a different kind. Let go of your busy mind. You don't have to always be right. Open your eyes and your heart to learn new ways of being, for there is so much to see. Steal a kiss and you will remember what you miss. Hafiz knows the dervish is free to face the challenges as they come. Put away your list of rules and follow the light of the lantern of hope. Be true to what you feel is real. An Oracle comes to help you, for now is the time to discover your divine power!

MANTRA

I am open to seeking new ways to revive and renew my energy and live fully and joyfully!

SONG OF SILENCE

Quiet your mind to hear divine whispers.

*Better not to reveal my pain
to false healers for I am
hoping to receive a remedy
from the hidden source.*

HAFIZ

There is an exquisite, natural sanctuary that shelters the treasures within you. It is the sacred silence that guards the pearl of divine wisdom, which has been gifted to you from birth. Hafiz is an Oracle and friend who lights your path to this source. Follow his advice; turn inward to rest and center within. Move your attention and focus beyond your inner dialogue, and discover the sacred healing that leads you to peace.

Hafiz is encouraging you to enter into your own interior energy and draw creatively from the wholeness of your being. Learn to experience the wonderful value of silence through carefully grounding your precious thoughts instead of talking ceaselessly to others. Seek your solutions within, paying more attention to the divine whispers of spirit and mystical wisdom. Place these moments as the sacred hours with your heart. Enter the kingdom of silence and meet your own higher truth — it is here that you will find your personal power.

MANTRA

I retreat from distracting thoughts to discover the beauty and power within me.

SONG OF SUCCESS
Dare to do what you love.

*Thank God, my midnight cries
and morning sighs were not in vain.
Every drop of those lustful tears
turned into a precious pearl.*

HAFIZ

Hafiz is a wisdom Oracle who comes to share a precious secret with you — success in life is doing what you truly love to do. Open your heart and listen to the desires hidden there. The revelations will guide your path to express and manifest these truths. Hafiz sings of the sweet triumph that rises as midnight cries of the longing for love, and the morning sighs to help you create it. This is the empowering energy that unlocks the vision of embracing the beloved.

Dear one, organize and use your time more wisely. Achieve your grace and wholeness through communion with the beauty of who you truly are. Pursue the opportunities that can bring blessings to you. If you want to enjoy the journey, use your leadership skills, as well as the skills and experiences of other people who can help you along the way. Go after achieving the dream that has been cradled in your heart for so long. Follow the golden rays that light your way and feel the serenity that pure love brings you. Walk lightly, taking one step at a time into the delight of a new life until you reach the success of your dreams.

MANTRA
I will follow my heart to achieve my greatest vision for success.

SONG OF SURRENDER

Follow the caring love that seeks your freedom.

*The more you feel divine love,
the more you surrender,
for you begin to feel the
tender beloved within you.*

HAFIZ

You have been created with an inner strength that needs to manifest on an outer level. By surrendering to that power, you'll be able to resolve many of the issues you may be facing in life. Notice how nature effortlessly produces everything through surrendering. A seed grows into a tall tree only through submission. You can similarly activate the power within you to attract and create your desired wishes.

Hafiz is a dear friend who inspires you to have more trust in the capable hand that guides your course in a profoundly desirable way. He is encouraging you to surrender to the caring love that seeks your freedom. Receive the oracle as a gift and a grace that is awakening you to your own inner wisdom. Trust the voice within you with total consent, and have the assurance that your choice is the right one in any given situation. Accept surrender as power — draw on your inner strength with joy, and grow into the consciousness of the wonder of who you are!

MANTRA
I surrender to the guiding hand of life to move me toward achieving my dream.

SONG OF UNIQUENESS

Look within to find your authentic identity.

*Dear heart, when looking for grandeur,
search within for its essence.
This I heard from a master
with great insight and presence.*

HAFIZ

Everything in existence is unique; nothing in the universe duplicates another. Quoting a master with great awareness, Hafiz brings you an important insight into the art of living: The personality of everyone springs from their heart. If you want to find your uniqueness, look inside. The deeper you reach into the well of your own soul, the more you can draw from it.

Dearest! Be bold and live life on your own terms. To live a unique life, you have to shed the fear of being wrong. Know that you are so much more than you have been taught to believe you are. Your first duty is now to yourself. Trust your heart and seek your own counsel. Rely on your inner values rather than social opinions. Through listening to your heart and using your imagination to express it, you will be able to generate new and unique ideas that are practical. By following through, your intuition will grow stronger and you will build your confidence as a master of self. From then on, you will always sense and know the correct decision to create the path to follow in your own unique way.

MANTRA
I will rely on my unique features to set the stage for my newly emerging life.

ABOUT THE AUTHOR & ARTIST

Rassouli is an artist, author, and inspirational guide who has dedicated his life to illuminating the path to happiness, fulfillment, and tranquility regardless of circumstances. He lives in Southern California, but his spirit is at home dancing around a canvas to bring paintings to life, watching the sunrise to find inspiration for writing books and essays on mysticism, and channeling kindred spirits to receive revelations for sharing with spiritual seekers in countless ways.

Rassouli's works reflect the shifting light and color of love and express the alchemy of this transformative energy in his visionary ways. He shares the mystical awareness in which he lives, reflects the streaming vibrations of the playfulness of the sages, and illuminates the messages of the great oracles of the world. His guidance is grounded in the gaze of the beloved as he lives the vigil of love through a surrendered heart.

Within the past four decades, Rassouli has exhibited worldwide, authored a dozen inspirational books and oracle decks, and lectured across the globe on the art of living. He has guided others in retreats, where he has shared his approach on how best to live with serenity and joy in delightfully pragmatic ways.

www.rassouli.com
www.avatarfinearts.com
www.freydoonrassouli.com
www.newdawncollections.com

Also available from Blue Angel Publishing®

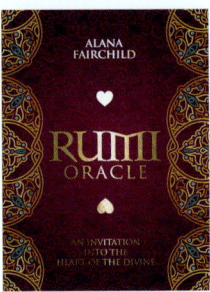

RUMI ORACLE
An Invitation into the Heart of the Divine

Alana Fairchild
Artwork and Rumi poetry translations by Rassouli

Rumi speaks a sacred language that we understand with our hearts rather than our minds. He knows the heart is the gateway to divine union and he doesn't want you to play small this lifetime. He encourages humanity to live and love with absolute surrender, abandon and willingness to accept the mysteries of life.

Whether you have studied his poetry for years or are drawn to him only now, this oracle deck will strengthen and illuminate your connection with this beautiful and powerful soul who loves you with a fierce passion.

ISBN: 978-1-922161-68-0
44 cards and 204-page guidebook.

Also available from Blue Angel Publishing®

GREAT EASTERN ORACLE
Empowering Guidance of the Mystics from Ancient to Modern Times

Rassouli

Explore the divine philosophies of forty mystics through the wonder, brilliance, and artistry of Rassouli. Enliven your greater truth, open secret doors, and wander into beauty, inspiration, and spiritual enrichment as you journey into the hearts and wisdom of Confucius, Gurdjieff, Rumi, Gibran, and more.

    A potent combination of visual and textual cues, each card holds a thousand interpretations and unlocks even more possibilities. Go beyond the rational to a place where potential evolves and your passions, values, and loves are at the center of your unfolding narrative.

ISBN: 978-1-922573-19-3
44 cards and 176-page guidebook.

Also available from Blue Angel Publishing®

SOUL'S JOURNEY ORACLE
Practical Epiphany for Personal Growth

Rassouli

Open your heart to the mysterious beauty of this oracle to seed and grow radiant contentment as you realize your unique destiny. Rassouli's enchanted messages, mantras, and artwork are interlaced with love, wisdom, and inspiration to nurture, guide, and uplift your soul. Turn to the wonders of divine creativity and practical epiphany to light up the dreams, treasures, secrets, and possibilities of your Soul's Journey.

"Oracles speak to us through metaphor and magic. We connect with them through our imaginations. In creating this deck, I surrendered to my inner calling to allow divine wisdom to speak directly to every open heart." – Rassouli

ISBN: 978-1-922573-88-9
44 cards and 120-page guidebook.

Also available from Blue Angel Publishing®

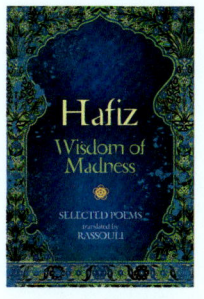

HAFIZ: WISDOM OF MADNESS
Selected Poems

Translated by Rassouli

Described as a literary wonder and a poet for poets, Hafiz has been lauded by Emerson, Goethe, Brahms, and Nietzsche. Now, renowned artist and writer, Rassouli has dived heart first into the "Divan of Hafiz" to offer you fresh, careful and devoted translations so you can take your own journey into the "Wisdom of Madness". The treasures of Hafiz will bless the reader for a lifetime.

Includes illustrations by Rassouli.

ISBN: 978-1-925538-64-9
204 pages, paperback book.

Also available from Blue Angel Publishing®

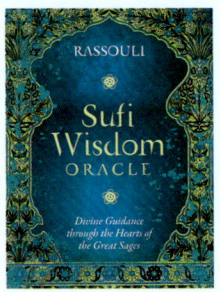

SUFI WISDOM ORACLE
Divine Guidance through the Hearts of the Great Sages

Rassouli

Experience the alchemical wisdom of history's most influential Sufi sages with this true work of devotion from esteemed artist, author, and teacher Rassouli. His glorious imagery, insightful commentary, and direct translations from the Persian texts create a window into the rich and numinous world of Sufism. Discover your soul purpose, make empowering choices, trust your intuition, have more satisfying relationships, and develop awareness, creativity, love, and more.

Each of the 44 cards depicts the Sufi message that appeared on Rassouli's canvas as he surrendered to his higher consciousness. The 164-page guidebook introduces you to fifteen mystics whose messages are like friends from the higher realms and have the spirit to empower and inspire you.

ISBN: 978-1-925538-65-6
44 cards and 164-page guidebook.

Also available from Blue Angel Publishing®

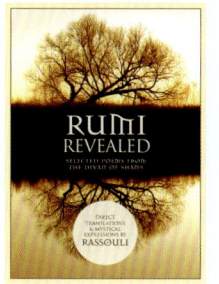

RUMI REVEALED
Selected Poems from the Divan of Shams

Direct Translations & Mystical Expressions by Rassouli

Rumi has been introduced to the western world primarily as a poet, but the scope of his creative power and the range of his vision shine far beyond the literary genre of poetry. Rumi was often in an exalted state when he shared the revelations of his poetic expression. Playing a sitar and singing and dancing his joy wherever he went, Rumi exhibited a tireless energy to proclaim the unlimited potential of the human being.

In *Rumi Revealed*, mystic artist and author Rassouli, who was raised as a Sufi, reveals the deeper essence of Rumi through his direct translations and visionary interpretations of Rumi's ecstatic verses.

ISBN: 978-1-922161-38-3
260 pages, paperback book.

For more information on this
or any Blue Angel Publishing® release,
please visit our website at:

www.blueangelonline.com